To Susan a~
Enjoy! This is my gift
to your trip - (get Susan to
tell you of our time together
at Margaret's party this
Summer in Albequerque.)
OK. I exaggerate ... but
I think you'll like her poetry!

Love
Jesse X
8/19/88

Susan
    Lizard poem page 37

(smile)
there are many metaphors
for this love we share
so many things
for us to be

MEMORY SAYS YES

by

MARGARET RANDALL

CURBSTONE PRESS

Cover design by Barbara Byers
Cover photograph by Colleen McKay

printed in the United States
by Curbstone Press

The production of this book was funded in part by The Connecticut
Commission on the Arts, a State agency whose funds are recommended
by the Governor and appropriated by the State Legislature, and in part
by the generous contribution of numerous individuals.

Some of these poems have appeared in AGAINST THE CURRENT,
THE AMERICAN VOICE, AMERICAS REVIEW, BERKELEY POETRY
REVIEW, CALAPOOYA COLLAGE, CALYX, CLOCKWATCH
REVIEW, CONCEPTIONS SOUTHWEST, CONDITIONS,
CONNECTICUT POETRY, HERESIES, IKON, LATIN AMERICAN
PERSPECTIVES, LITERARY ARTS HAWAII, NEW DIMENSIONS,
NEW LETTERS, O. ARS, and THIRD RAIL. A *Poetry of Resistance*,
Participatory Research Group, Toronto, 1983 first published "All Last
Week" under the previous title of "March 6, 1982." Several are part of
Albuquerque: Coming back to the USA, New Star Books, Vancouver,
1986. Some also appeared in a pamphlet called *The Coming Home
Poems*, which was published by Long River Books, East Haven,
Connecticut in 1986 to benefit the Margaret Randall Legal Defense
Committee. "Killing the Saint," "The Second Photograph," "Guilty of
Innocence," and "Coatlicue" are part of the collection *This Is About
Incest*, Firebrand Books, Ithaca, New York, 1987. Salient Seedling
Press, Brooklyn, New York, printed "Talk to Me" as a broadside also
benefitting the Margaret Randall Legal Defense Fund.

ISBN: 0-915306-77-8
LC Number: 87-73442

distributed in the United States by
THE TALMAN COMPANY
150 Fifth Avenue
New York, NY 10011

CURBSTONE PRESS, 321 Jackson Street, Willimantic, CT 06226

this book is for Barbara

PREFATORY NOTE

Margaret Randall is among those most endearing artists who choose/dare to express political sensibility in poetry of the heart.

* * *

Memory Says Yes is not a lecture in verse. It is Margaret's own mantra we hear. In poem after poem she confronts straight on the all-too-real nightmares that have invaded her own life.

* * *

Margaret is my friend. I know she believes that we are part of the celebration of one world, one heart. But if we get the pleasure of that magnificent union, we must also see ourselves as included in the tragedy. "We hold the infamy, all of us hold the infamy in our hands."

* * *

Above all, her moving poetry challenges apathy, indifference, inaction and fear. She writes, "Do it. That's all. Please. No more questions. No more knowledgeable statements. Three words. Begin a poem. Take your life and use it." Dear Margaret, in my own life, I find *that* to be the morning call.

She writes, "I have two voices, tongues, with which to ask and say. Sometimes my Latino high lilts against the gutteral deepness of my Jewish shadowland." . . . . and Margaret, it is the harmony you create that offers us such a rich song.

— Holly Near

V

TABLE OF CONTENTS

MEMORY SAYS YES

UNDER THE STAIRS

My childhood place beneath the family's stairs
was home to Mr. Beeuff, Miss Level, Camp, Girlie—
faithful friends who came
when there was no one else.
Instantly available, invisible to eyes
unprimed to take them in
or on.

We talked endlessly then
through years when Radio let imagination live
and presidents still died natural deaths.

Mr. Beeuff and Miss Level were adults. Ageless
in maturity and sedentary power.
His lined face and lunch pail.
She a nurse in crisp white service.
Years, then, of righteous wars, defense plants
and defense of honor.
Her hands were always clean.

Camp wore a leather jacket, rode a motorcycle,
was my male hero. Power and comfort
in the same breath.
Girlie was just that, *his* girl,
pliant, pretty in whatever image of pretty
lit my eight-year-old eyes.
"No ideas but in things," Williams would say,
but what of ourselves as things? What about service?

When I asked about Pearl Harbor
my friends told me wars were o.k.
Not to worry, as the saying goes. Today,
my own wars vying for room inside my chest,
I trace murky reason to those ready answers.

My body is just now my own. My pain
sits toward the back of the theatre. Chewing its nails.

Roque rides a bus, heavy volume of Che
on his jostling lap. He laughs.
How often now has the thousand dollars for Alvaro
changed hands?
Alvaro, Jose Benito,
interchangeable names in the single focus of death.

Liz says it's true, years ago she was shy
and had to work hard to bridge the deficit.
Debts never cancelled somehow, debtors
still looking for a place to stand up,
a place to say: I am.
When the body goes, can we say our work is done?

Mr. Beeuf might be a P-Niner now, his lunch pail
tired of the old liverwurst sandwiches,
pickles and chips.
Miss Level will not deal well
with memories of raging skin, pieces of bodies
cracking her memory
after Korea. After Vietnam. El Salvador.
Camp chooses himself. Girlie remains size eight.

Carlos' blue eyes pierce my poem,
Violeta's wound opens again and again
in my own right temple.
Light fades from Havana's seawall, brightens
over my mountain, whimpers in my hands.

We are always going home, going home
wherever memory stands up, says
it's time now. Right now it's time.

On days like these I take the silence
and the sweetness of these men and women
crowding my memory
waking through the cold of that
which is empty, unfinished.
I grab their breath, their teeth,
and tell them what I've learned:

It's not true
a child has no memory before the age of two.
You cannot solve the problems of the planet
in the space for lovers
but lovers can live in the world
if they work at it.
Dignity has bone, muscle.
There is no such thing as absolute truth.

We talk awhile, under the stairs.
I talk and listen as I did then.
They come and go as then.

Albuquerque, Summer 1987

13

THE GLOVES

for Rhoda Waller

Yes we did march around somewhere and yes it was cold,
we shared our gloves because we had a pair between us
and a New York City cop also shared his big gloves with me
– strange, he was there to keep our order
and he could do that and I could take that
back then.

We were marching for the Santa Maria, Rhoda,
a Portuguese ship whose crew had mutinied.
They demanded asylum in Goulart's Brazil
and we marched in support of that demand
in winter, in New York City, back and forth
before the Portuguese consulate,
Rockefeller Center, 1961.
I gauge the date by my first child
– Gregory was born late in 1960 – as I gauge
so many dates by the first, the second, the third, the fourth,
and I feel his body now, again, close to my breast,
held against cold to our strong steps of dignity.

That was my first public protest, Rhoda,
strange you should retrieve it now
in a letter out of this love of ours
alive these many years.
How many protests since that one, how many
marches and rallies
for greater causes, larger wars, deeper wounds
cleansed or untouched by our rage.

Today a cop would hardly unbuckle his gloves
and press them around my blue-red hands.

14

Today a baby held to breast
would be a child of my child, a generation removed.
The world is older and I in it
am older,
burning, slower, with the same passions.
The passions are older and so I am also younger
for knowing them more deeply and moving in them
pregnant with fear
but fighting.

The gloves are still there, in the cold,
passing from hand to hand.

Albuquerque, March 1985

LETTER FROM MANAGUA / one

All you want to do is murder us, those who have survived
your several dress rehearsals.
It's not that serious yet, most of us don't meet
your person-level, neither robust nor blue-eyed
nor promising according to your current IQ
the rorschach that defines your sense of life.
Forgive us if we don't agree
with your definition of the N-bomb
the binary chemical solution or the Salvadoran solution
as an adequate pain-killer.
We're sufficiently underdeveloped
to want to deal with our pain
in our own primitive way. Forgive us too
if we can't fully answer your questions
about our society, define it
as marxist-leninist or social democrat,
agreeably pluralist or sufficiently free enterprise,
if we insist on the crudity
of exploring our own creative process
loving our homeland
with the passion 50,000 sisters and brothers
root in our throats.
Excuse us, please, we're always forgetting
we were supposed to ask permission
to defend our truth
and distribute our laughter as we see fit.
Don't bother yourselves trying to understand
our teaching our soldiers poetry along with defense combat
self-respect and how to write their names
in ink instead of blood.
When our grandparents scraped their living from this land
you sent your marines.
Later you provided us with one of our own,

he had a brother and a son, a grandson
and infinite pockets.
We said goodbye more than once
but you trained a legion of our brothers
bought them and kept them in shape
to keep us in shape
and the shape they kept us in was increasingly pine-boxed
and horizontal.
Here it was a crime to be young
and you reminded us daily of that crime
committed by so many and so often.
But we kept forgetting.
We fought and came up
from under your undying friend
and his protective Guard.
We fought and won, we buried
our sisters and brothers (few were blond
or met your standards for personhood)
and we began the long pain, the silent joy,
the impossible made possible
our history of eyes and hands.
We know we don't meet your general 1982 guidelines
for dependent nations.
All you want to do is murder us.
All we want to do is live.

Managua, February 1982

17

LETTER FROM MANAGUA / two

I no longer felt the heat or pain
when the photograher put me on film
in 1978.
The charred black mass of my body
was only the limited space of another life.
A spark moved voids in that image
and I emerged
radiant, whole
in the conscionesness my dark remains evoked
in an old woman in Lima, a teenager on Chicago's south side,
a London poet, students in Canberra, a guerrilla in Morazan.

But my temperature rose
searing Haig's lying hands
when he held me up to damn my sisters and brothers,
betray those who fought and fell
and were born with me
that long September day.
In our new state we can only be used for life, not death
nor to justify those who would go on burning
our names and eyes.

Now I suffer for earth and water,
fire and air.
Only by snuffing out the napalm in Beirut,
reviving the peasant girl in Vietnam's smile
washing the blood from the streets of Chalatenango,
the Bronx, Santiago, San Francisco Norte, Belfast, San Juan,
will I be able to sleep
in love, at rest, alert.

Managua, July 1982

18

ALL LAST WEEK

for my daughter, Ana

All last week you preened before the mirror
viewing emerging breasts, then covering them
with gauze-thin blouse
and grinning: getting bigger, huh?

The week before you wore army fatigues
leveling breasts and teenage freckles,
tawny fuzz along your legs. A woman. Beginning.

Today you don fatigues again.
Today you pack knapsack and canteen,
lace boots over heavy socks
and answer the call Reagan and Haig
have slung at your 12 years.

Yours and so many others
– kids 14, 15, 18, so many others who will go
and some of them stay, their mothers
shouting before the Honduran Embassy:
"Give us our sons' bodies back,
give us back their bodies!" At least that.

All last week you preened before the mirror,
moving loose to new rhythms
long weekend nights. Junior High math. Sunday beach.
Today you go off
to the stacatto of continuous news dispatches.
And I, in my trench, carry your young breasts
in my proud and lonely eyes.

Managua, March 1982

A MAN HAS GONE BACK

for Julio Cortazar

A man has gone back to his city, a place
some have told him cannot be recognized
in its great new structures
glass and steel
rising where the edge of the world
meets his eye.

He thinks of this
coming from where
the magic bird has set him down.
But the smell of grilled meat
at construction sites
stays in the workers' shirts,
tells him he's home.

Thirty thousand walk these streets
profiles snap full-face
where the heat of a body
memorized this bench, this park,
and each particular way of saying hello
continues to claim our skin.

Thirty thousand shadows
change this city forever,
these minutes, days, never again to be new.

He has gone back.
He walks these streets in desperate company.

Managua, January 1984

20

LIKE BEADS

for Floyce Alexander

There is something stuck in my laughter
language worn thin by summers, churning.

The steadiness of your eyes
calms me.

I weep for a lost hand, the knuckles
taut against old bone.
I weep for hearts and livers,
piles of gold teeth, mountains of hair.

A woman stares at the eye
gouged from her brother's human face,
my fist-sized muscle
thunders against your voice.

Time becomes old words, then shatters
as we walk through
planting our feet on sand that moves.

Days to be counted off the round stone
like beads in the hand
of a woman who photographs her own death.

A scenario replayed against Managua's open fields,
against her mouth, a wound.

I speak to you now from the Margaret in my throat.

Managua, December 1983

21

GET GOING

for Floyce Alexander

Splice the smile, get going
under an arch of time
where memory rips pictures
(felt-backed figures on a board)
and something as yet unknown
rips memory. Holds it. Rips it.

Salvation in anger.
Sorrow leading to fear.
The tight-fitting shirt
has no place against this breast
fighting to breathe. To be open.

No performance at sundown.
This gift the greatest glory:
no performance, but man
opening and touching. Letting me in.
Offering his memory of future.

I will take time
in both hands, knead it
and roll it out.
Gather and bring it in once more.
I will part the bread as I see fit,
put some away for yesterday, make tomorrow
as long and full as I want.

No. Not as I want. As I need.
As long and full as I need.

Albuquerque, June 1984

22

STAR 80

The man on the screen was going to be someone
using the woman on the screen.
the man on the screen photographed a delectible object
endlessly.
(With me it was always partial. Partial.)
The mother knew but her eyes vanished.
The man on the screen invented and blundered,
then need cruised his body and he bought a pardon.
(In my life it always seemed more like reality. So subtle.)
The woman on the screen saw herself changing according to the rules
and travelled an old road. The sun came out. Briefly.
Then the man without a history bought a gun.
Everything had already happened
as many times as there are pores in my body.
And it happened again.
Pity occupied another house.
The sound was explosive and final.

I sat very still.
They pushed my head against the seat hard.
My hands grew cold. Then hot.
In each of my body's pores
memory lit a single candle.
Wax smothered the pore.
Still, I burned.
Pain moved like music
as each receding image
filled with my exact experience.
I felt old from so much pain.
In my seat I did not want to rise.
I wanted to wait for the answer.

Albuquerque, February 1984

MYSELF, REGROUPING

These are my hands. Here they are.
Good hands, large and strong.
Hands that have written poems
brought children to the world,
made love and war.
In dreams they often race
or grow beyond their boundaries.
In dreams they have been black
as well as cold.

These are my feet. Also large.
Spread flattened for years in crude sandals.
Lately, through re-entry,
shod with intimidating boots.
I like the intimidation.
It balances the smiles.

This is my smile. Sometimes
it fears exposure,
more often it breaks and tumbles
beyond the confines of my mouth.
In your mouth's upturned corners
it has found a friend.

Tongue to tongue. Tooth to tooth.
When your smile comes small and stops
mine longs to move in close,
hold and complete your process.
I have strong legs, thighs that seize and clasp,
broad hips belly breasts
marked by babies and by years.
Elbows that seldom wait by windows anymore
but often stump a silent keyboard
caress their own body's fingers holding myself.

My fingers. They are light-sensitive
and live in history's mouth.
My nose has been called patrician by some,
elephant snout by a boy in seventh grade
whose taunt I'm only now forgetting.
My hair has been braided dark brown
teased in the hesitant years
dyed a while in the bridging years, reclaiming
its silver fire.

I have been told my eyes can see
and yes, they can.
They see and see and sometimes do not close
even when I will them to.
A third eye opens and shuts around my neck,
my camera's lens
ready and waiting on my skin.

I have two voices, tongues with which to ask and say.
Sometimes my Latina high lilts against the gutteral deepness
of my Jewish shadowland.
A questioning Spanish "no?" moves restless
through reclaimed English
 – Seville, Mexico, Havana, Lima, Hanoi, Managua,
Scarsdale, Lower East Side, Albuquerque, everywhere.

My ears are less than perfect
inherited with love from my father
(as are my gums).
My memory shreds.
Memory . . . The hardest part.
So easy to lose. So distant or so close.
Lately I spend half my life trying to remember.
Four children, extensions of myself
though not possessed nor held by me.
Their own eyes and hands, their own feet

travel them out as they return
completing my voice, a circle turning.

This is the skin I shed
and the new one
pulling against my bones.
This is my pain.
I claim it too
and offer it along with deepest love
as gift and remedy.

Albuquerque, March 1985

REMAINING OPTION

I

My temperature goes up
and "who can measure the heat and violence
of the poet's heart
when caught in a woman's body?"
Virginia Woolf asked that
and went to sleep in her cold river.
Sexton and Plath, Santamaría and Parra
left abruptly
breaking the barrier of heat as someone or something
called in a voice louder than the heart.

Sexton started me down this road today
telling me Ann Frank was the Joan of Arc of Amsterdam.
A different kind of death.
And Ronnie Gilbert, singing
"The water is wide . . . I cannot cross."
It *is* wide but I *can* cross,
am crossing now, falling against the waves,
hoisting myself aboard the craft once more, going on.
Wet but warmed to this place
where a lagging heat divides and pulls me together again.

II

On the silver road last night
I stopped my car.
Stopped and pulled over, pulling my body
into its own curve,
hugging arms, thighs, ribs.
A shoulder was caught in the silent blade
of my windshield wiper.

The night was calm.
Fingers splayed against the glass
and the ancient bridle of an 18th century mount
was crushed beneath the front wheel
when I emerged desperate for air.

These are the fingers of war, the shoulders of war,
the bridle of unjust death,
fragments of fear.
These pieces of my mind
that will not stay behind
nor wilt.

III

Temperature and music
make room for the heart.
Memory presses against canyon walls
chipping the dark side of flight.

I am crossing now. Oh yes,
I am crossing.

Albuquerque, April 1985

KILLING THE SAINT

Your father   my grandfather   the saint
the parts of his body
are taking back their names.
Once you said yes, maybe
he also forced my brother. Maybe he forced me.

But now again you don't remember.
I didn't say that, you tell me tonight.
I never said that.
Flashes of mirror pinning wet clothes
to a line in moonlight. Fear.

Mother you are larger now.
Awkward we split. The mirror goes.

A year passes and another, we don't
talk about these things (we
who are so close)
we don't say these things
without a neat period, sufficient commas.

Then one day I use the hard-won memory,
sit before you, and begin.
You say the right thing.
It has taken me years to understand
your answers are often that: words
speaking to themselves.
Words moving in unison
put a good face forward. Everyone claps.

Mother when your demons loom
and you become larger than life
my children grow small on that horizon.

As you pull I lose them one by one.
Or is it me I lose?
Or is it me I fear to lose?

In this poem I hold your eyes and shout
please mother, don't say the words you think we want.
Speak from your own fear.

Look, I am bringing my children back, circling their size.
Killing the saint in his thirty years of death.

Touching the rotten flesh in moonlight.
Watching the pillars fall. Retrieving their pieces.

Albuquerque, Spring 1986

THE SECOND PHOTOGRAPH

I have found another portrait.
You have me on your lap
flanked by my two grandmothers
both looking congenitally worried
as well they should.

You, on the other hand, seem vaguely crazed
as you certainly were,
your lips and eyes focused on different planes.

I have looked long and hard
at the hands in this picture.
Both women hide theirs, differently.
Yours, Grandpa, are loosely circled
about my three-year-old body.
Your right covers my left, your left
comes round my party-dressed buttocks,
your fingers strangely held as if in secret sign.

I am reading this into the image.
I am reading it because now, half a century later,
I understand why my eyes in the picture
take the camera head on, demanding answers.

                              Albuquerque, Spring 1986

31

SOMEONE TRUSTED HAS USED FORCE

The triangle veered
and fell.

From mother/father/child
to home/world/memory . . .
that's me.

Suddenly there are
infinite triangles:
Protect/evade/love,
Force/fear/shut down,
Mind/body/sex,
Lie/be safe/survive . . .

Look/lie/remember,
Retreat/forget/forget,
Comfort/close/fear,
Power/options/hope . . .

Earth/memory/sky,
Water/sky/memory,
Memory/earth/water . . .

Until there is fire
pushing earth and water apart,
sky searing the hands.

Sky burns
and the triangle
no longer holds the child
within familiar sides.

Someone trusted has used force
to enter this space.

Memory tears and shreds.
Life and memory
have both been sacrificed.

Nothing is as it was.

Albuquerque, Spring 1986

THE GREEN CLOTHES HAMPER

Rain almost hides my mountains today.
Low clouds snag the rocky skirts, colors
of rain and clouds clean everything.

I speak of the rain, the clouds, the living
colors of this land
because it seems impossible to cut this silence with the words

my grandfather was a sick and evil man
posing as healer.
Now I retrieve his hands and eyes, his penis
filling my tiny infant mouth

as he forced himself into a body, mine,
that still finds reason easier than feeling.
Here is the green lucite top
of a clothes hamper where rape impaled diapers.

Here is memory catching up with itself,
overtaking asthma, compulsive food, fear
of that which is *not* itself.
This lost green hamper. My body coming home.

                                    Albuquerque, Spring 1986

GUILTY OF INNOCENCE

The moon opens my palms, my hands
are full of the distance between themselves,
full with my first power.

My schoolyard's trees are larger now, their branches heavy,
a great shade. Memory stands up.
These trees once small as I was small.

My hands, their palms straining
against a loss of memory
(loss, no, we do not *lose* this image of our lives.
It is taken from us. Stolen. Raped.)

Abraham Bomba speaks.
"That night was the most horrible night for all the people,
because of the memory of all those things that people went
through with each other – all the joys and the happiness and
the births and the weddings and other things– and all of a
sudden, in one second, to cut through without anything, and
without any guilt of the people, because the people weren't
guilty at all. The only guilt they had was that they were
Jewish."
Abraham Bomba, survivor of Treblinka.

Daily suffocation, continuous beatings,
violation of trust, abuse and holocaust
wear the magnet thin, take power. Ours. Mine.
Hands empty at our sides, resignation stand-in for loss.

Jewish is not guilty.
Poor is not guilty.
Black is not guilty.
Being a child, being small

is not guilty.
Woman is not guilty.
Lesbian or gay man are not guilty.
Having a different body is not guilty.
Having different ideas is not guilty.

This plateau is a great and quiet place.
Cool breeze whips to wind, inflates the world between my
palms.
Take it slow, this is all you may want to do today
and the wanting
here in your hands
is strong, your process.

Motke Zaidl and Itzhak Dugin:
"When we first opened the graves, we couldn't help it, we all
burst out sobbing. But the Germans almost beat us to death. We
had to work at a killing pace . . . beaten all the time, and with
no tools. The Germans even forbade us to use the words corpse or
victim. The dead were blocks of wood, shit, with absolutely no
importance. Anyone who said corpse or victim was beaten. The
Germans made us refer to the bodies as *Figuren*, that is, as
puppets, as dolls, or as *Schmattes*, which means rags."
Motke Zaidl and Itzhak Dugin, survivors of Vilna.

The rape of language, the rape of meaning.
Guilty of innocence. Innocent guilt.
Memory hibernating
when memory threatens life.
Memory coming back returns survival.

Heal with these hands, which are yours. Yourself.
Remember with these hands
which are yours.

Albuquerque, Spring 1986

LIZARD

Even through the bad times
I always had an image,
something round and endless,
a room of our own.

Of course there would be more than one room
but it was the one shared
that flowered in gentle reassurance,
electricity and dream.
A place to be old.

You are not old together
when you are no longer lovers, you are not
eyes searching each other's eyes, hands
touching.

Loss of the tiny silver lizard broach
became a metaphor, *our* loss.
You found the lizard
its small ribcage faintly battered
by wash cycles, time.

Albuquerque, August 1986

WITH APOLOGIES TO NANCY DREW

"Just a case of mistaken identity . . .
ours was just a case . . . "
refrain or label, it does not feel
right for humans

who loved each other,
love themselves.
Who loved the struggle to love well,
the struggle to love each other
and themselves.

"Ours was just a case
of mistaken identity . . . nothing more.
You were not who I thought you were, I was
not who you wanted."

No thank you. I am who I am,
have always been. Not a case
of mistaken anything, not
a case . . . but myself.

Tell me you do not want to work it through
(I can hear that)
but note I have not given permission
for you or anyone
to mistake my identity.
Having only one, I intend to hold it.
Having only one, love is imperative. Thank you.

Albuquerque, Summer 1987

38

THE HEM OF MY SKIRT

Across the room I look at you
and smile.
You see a woman who walked a bridge
the hem of her skirt blackened, burnt.
It's me. It's my skirt. Come closer.
Yes I say it's a lovely day,
but the weather's changing.
You are talking to a woman with charred skirt
whose dried blood speaks to the moon.
No thanks, I've had enough.
Metaphor become rape, incest waking the dream.
A woman with charred skirt, open-ended moons, enduring hands.
You tell me to leave, my words threaten
to win one round in your plastic game.
You don't like the way I see. I *am* not sorry.
I am the loverless woman
no one to touch my ancient temples, longing spots
on either side of my skull.
Another drink? Yes, thanks . . .
I am the woman still crossing that bridge
skirt falling away in fire
whose sainted grandpa
took her for himself.
My blood dries on your hands.
I am this woman with teeth still sharp.
Neither lover nor country. Thank you.

San Diego/Albuquerque, Winter 1986

MEMORY SAYS YES

Morning unbends my body, opens my eyes, I hold you
across this continent
rubbing the voyage from your small square feet.

Balanced finely I turn
almost falling from the curb.
Now I banish need and want
pull the glow into my eyes
intercept your disappearance and stay
once more
in the slow heat of your flesh.

In my dream a bridge was built
an old car's brakes wouldn't hold
A Guatemalan holiday commemorated painful loss.

Perhaps the order is wrong. Memory bends when we sleep.
Light cuts time, reshuffles the deck,
we process the unexpected.
Two hours earlier
your voice will speak the next line.

Washington DC, June 1986

POLAR BEARS AND RABBIT WATCHING THE NORTHERN LIGHTS

(after a painting by Melissa Miller*)

The day just beginning to lighten the high windows was so distant, so grey. I settled into sleep once more, and almost immediately shook with a painful waking. The dream hung to my ribs and lips. I called you 500 miles away, in order to speak it out. In order to speak.

We slept in a warm, dark room. The house was very large, ample and replete with creature-comforts: appliances of different sorts, an outdoor hot-tub. In our room a sense of uneasiness began to shred the night. I climbed out of the bed, careful not to touch your sleep. Heading for the bathroom I saw your motorcycle, parked cleanly near the bedroom door.

I bypassed the bathroom, then, and wandered out towards the other rooms, leaving you behind. And Jane asleep in a large four-poster next to our own smaller, frame-futon. In a very modern kitchen I observed, astonished, knobs and switches in the semi-light. I remembered the first time I entered the kitchen at the Chaix home, Nicaragua 1980. After ten years of life in Cuba, the modernity simply stunned me. Immobility. Silence. Just about to put my hand out to touch a series of these, I felt everything beginning to shake. The earth shook. The house.

The room rocked, and a low rumbling filled me, ominous, terrifying. Then it was a roar. Louder. Engulfing my senses, the knobs and switches, the wall, the colors, and the shaking – which was at once a part of this rumbling destruction and in awkward opposition to it.

*Melissa Miller, b. 1951. *Northern Lights*, 1982. Oil on canvas. 66" x 74".

41

It was then that I heard you and Jane. Jane had come out of sleep to another bathroom, not enclosed within the communal sleeping space but positioned somewhere between that part of the house and the kitchen where I waited, terrified. Upon crossing the threshhold she screamed, and you had gone to her, quickly, competently. There the two of you were confronted by a fourth woman: Annie had killed herself.

Although I could distill no words from the vocal pain of your discovery, I somehow knew she was in the tub. Had she drowned? Perhaps. I tried then, and for centuries following the impact of that moment, to get to both of you, to move towards you – and her – in space. I tried but my legs would not work. I tried and I floated, never gaining ground, my arms and legs flailing as if in drugged water, trying, trying, desperate in my trying, enormous in my trying, too large, unwieldy, heavy and impotent in air that fought me all the way.

The noise was louder, and the world shaking itself free – of itself? – I did not know. I only knew at that moment I could not go where I needed to be, could not arrive, could not share in the solace of my dearest sisters. Death and a jarring movement, earth, thunder, the inability to move: these were the elements with which I woke.

I spoke to myself then, told myself how to unzip the portion of the canvas briefcase where the tiny telephone book waited. How to take the book, turn to the appropriate page, how to find and dial the number, how to listen for your voice and take it – as it answered – with joyous relief.

Tomorrow became, once more, the color of polar bears and rabbit, riveted on the northern lights. Icy whites containing blues and reds and yellows and so much blue and, yes, so much yellow. Sun, there in the north. There in the cold. Here in my heart. Even the black water, a comfort. We talked. We

practised the sacred art of talk. It was not about my friends, I
thought. Not about this place. It was December. My month.
Your voice eclipsed the miles. You were rocking me then.
Tomorrow exists. With all its colors.

Albuquerque, Winter 1986

BEAR LAKE

She mixed a dark palate at Bear Lake 1930,
reds and blacks and greys
but the reds are dark, it is all dark
and I stand once more in her shadow
straining to each brush each bringing forth
of muscle, a place to stay. Not hide.

She mixed her palate, unhidden, doing
everything against the rules. "No wonder
they hated her," you said.

I am not speaking to but about her, I address
us both.
She working the thirties, decade of my birth, I
entering, registering upon my eyes and hands
the life where I would work this hard
fight this hard
die this hard in the living.

"Come into the flower," she tells me,
"all the way in.
Touch the land, touch yourself."
These are words placed nowhere
but upon my living skin upon my lips
a place where memory stands.

Deep red contours, almost black, grey shadows
twisting out of this land,
my breath settles the magic streak of light.
White. Uncanny white.
Sky streak, water, light. Milk
in the image I hold half a century later

along that road going home. Always going home.
I too have returned
and Georgia has moved on.
Bear Lake stands in testament.*

Albuquerque, Winter 1987

*After a Georgia O'Keefe painting, "Bear Lake," oil on canvas, 30" X 40", 1930.

45

VARIATION ON THE DOOR

With Adrienne Rich

There is nothing I would not give
for years or even minutes,
time moving differently in this place we occupy,
memory hoisting itself upright in us.

There is nothing I would not give
you or another,
repetition comforts me today,
a long delicate line of pink light parts the sky
and a coyote crossing the road makes you smile.

Knowing you here – a here
distant as voices or a room apart
(working as I work)
our air becoming a single air –
knowing you here holds my body in space,
fixes my mind.

This knowledge neither linear nor perfect
is again and again the door
opening because we have chosen
to walk through, chosen to risk,
remember our names.

Memory walks tall in this dream, memory
and hope.
Nothing can call me home, love,
but to your eyes and hands.

Albuquerque, Winter 1987

46

THE DAY WE FOUND THE RINGS

I knew where
but not the face of what we would see there.
We did not find it
and left, confused but undiminished.
You saw the bear's claw, then,
turned its memory in your own
and we returned along a road
trading us patience for trust.

The rings were persistent
pulling our fingers into their circles of heat.

We had help. From the voices
still moving in those shadows
as they sound on canyon walls,
from the storytellers, the keepers of vision,
Mary Colter,*
women whose silent lives repeat themselves in us.

And from the bears
who place one foot before the other.

Grand Canyon/Albuquerque, Winter 1987

*Mary Colter (1869-1958) was an architect and interior designer who loved and
understood the Indians of the North American Southwest. She produced her
best-known work for the Fred Harvey Company, manager of the most important
concessions along the Santa Fe Railway line when it opened the West in the
early years of this century. Hopi House, the place where these rings were
waiting, was built by her on the Grand Canyon's south rim in 1905.

I WILL NAME IT

I will name it, safely I will
step on its toes, cause it
to stand still in my hand
turning its eyes to look towards mine.

I will give it a name
with wings of brilliant blue,
a name with proud letters,
deep sound.

Its name will live through and beyond
these broken years
sleep in the hollow of your neck,
warmed in the curve of your breast.

It will change language itself
this name of mine, fierce and sweet,
birthing new words where eyes and lips
repeat themselves in space.

It will change pain and fear, shivering nights
of burnt-out dream.
Whoever speaks this name will grow and sing.

Nothing lost to the straight of her neck,
to the strong calm of her hand.
Nothing riddled with bullets or with lies.

This name holds noun and verb,
a precious history.
This name of ours. Unspoken. Claimed. Complete.

Albuquerque, Winter 1987

WHEN IT SNOWS LIKE THIS

When it snows like this I cannot see my mountains.
The city is gone, time warps about me
a cloak of sunsets, color singing itself to sleep.

Night speaks a fearful language
but I have plucked from it "you must . . . you really should . . .
you are good enough, or much too good."

I take the lady with her scales by surprise.
Neither option warms my hands, lights my eyes, my voice.
I tie the lady's wrists behind her back.

Virgin or slut, sea urchin hoisting banners of blood
upon the land. I know my mountains
are here, still, my city hungry for a bridge.

I build that bridge now, stone upon stone,
reed upon reed, flag upon flag. Seaweed and sage,
then walk across it to the other side.
Walk across it, sisters, to the other side.

                              Albuquerque, Winter 1987

UNDER ATTACK

for Marian McDonald

Listen. These voices are under attack.

Ismaela of the dark tobacco house. Grandma.
A maid her lifetime of winters, granddaughter of slaves.
Straight to my eyes:
"my mama used to tell me, one of these days
the hens gonna shit upwards!
And I'd stare at those hens' asses, wondering
when *will* that happen?
When we pushed the big ones down
and pulled the little ones up!"

"For Mama, Papa, and Blackie" she wrote
on the poem she left to say goodbye.
Nicaragua, 1977.
Disappear or be disappeared.
Dora María whose gaze
her mother always knew.
She trembled at her first delivery,
then took a city fearlessly.

Rain and the river rising. Catalina
chases her ducks that stray.
"And my months," she cries,
on that platform with poles, a house
to do over and over.
"My months gone in the hospital at Iquitos
and the full moon
bringing a madness to my head."
Her body is light against my touch.
A woman's voice, parting such density of rain.

Xuan, my cold hands in hers,
evokes the barracks.
"Soldiers who were our brothers."
Night after night, village by village.
Quang Tri, 1974.
Gunfire replaced by quiet conversation.
The work of women.
Xuan's history, too, is under attack.

Dominga brings her memory down
from the needle trade, Don Pedro,
her own babies dead from hunger.
"I want to tell you my story," she says,
"leave it to the young ones
so they'll know."
We are rocking. We are laughing.
This woman who rescued the flag at Ponce,
Puerto Rico, 1937.
Known by that act alone,
until a book carries her words. Her voice.

I bring you these woman. Listen.
They speak, but their lives are under attack.

They too are denied adjustment of status
in the land of the free. In the home of the brave.

                          Albuquerque, Winter 1986

IMMIGRATION LAW

When I ask the experts
"how much time do I have?"
I don't want an answer
in years or arguments.

I must know
if there are hours enough
to mend this relationship,
see a book all the way to its birthing,
stand beside my father
on his journey.

I want to know how many seasons of chamisa
will be yellow then grey-green
and yellow
                /light/
                        again,
how many red cactus flowers
will bloom beside my door.

I will not follow language
like a dog with its tail between its legs.

I need time equated with music,
hours rising in bread.
years deep from connections.

The present always holds a tremor of the past.

Give me a handful of future
to rub against my lips.

                            Albuquerque, October 1985

52

TALK TO ME

Talk to me. Three words
moving with heavy feet
across the open spaces.

A signal,
or the beginning of a poem.

Talk to me. Not meaning
"how are things going?"
Not meaning
"they *can't* do this to you"
(they can, they are)
not even
"What can I do to help?"

Do it, that's all.
Please.
No more questions, no more
knowledgeable statements.

Three words. Begin a poem. Take your life
and use it.

Albuquerque, Winter 1986

THESE OUR HANDS

for Gina Talandis

Mother I wanted to tell you
who I am.

You crossed an ocean.
Fitting in
being like the ads
a blue sky   memories grafted   ə skin
that never quite took.

I said
look at me.
Your only words
made us sorry.

I hold the cloth
of time-bleached threads.
From great-grandmother's hands
from grandmother's hands
mother in a place without options.

They keep telling me
the options are two.
Love me or hate me.
Accept or reject.

There are other options.
I am fashioning them now
with these our hands.

Albuquerque, Winter 1986

54

HORIZON

Sharp line
separates ridge from dawn.
Colors,
almost before they become.

Separation of Church and State, I think,
of youth and age,
the lie and its particular truth.

Of course not.

Any one of the opponents
as much alike
as our bodies pressed together
reflection and will.

The game's up.

I am where I must be,
sun warms this house, slowly.

Something indelible has happened
on the land.

Albuquerque, Winter 1986

LITANY

for Jane Caputi

Couldn't happen here not here not to us
our rainbow in the sky
perfect teacher perfect Black
successful screen sudden break its twisted smoke
not here not us not in America
a president shot another and another
a president lying the leader snagged
in deceitful tapes
not here not now
a president who didn't duck
the Marlboro Man the actor of them all
not in America the perfect product the product packaged
headache relief at bedtime cyanide death at dawn
the computer doesn't lie not here not to us
America can't be wrong
your skirt must have been too short
too short too tight seduction is your crime
no real danger here
where the horse comes over the hill
where the man pushes back his hat.

Albuquerque, Winter 1986

ELECTION NOTES

On the TV screen they give us a play by play
of the wrong men being elected, it is we
who elect them
as we hold each other
trembling
you saying you feel crazy
pushing me away each time things are good.

Blood pounds late between my legs
and winter closes in,
even the deepest wood in the pile
is snow-wet all the way down.
On the TV screen statistics become images,
automatic satisfaction, numbers
fadeout to smiling faces.

Each political party has its own color,
no link with my private image-colors:
the number five cafe-au-lait,
my Margaret-name deep red,
green holding soon or safe,
and the pale yellow of light touch.
Almost everything used in kitchens turns black.

Yesterday in *my* kitchen
I kneaded bread, worked the dough
to unloose patience and sunsets,
a tight chest, the pain
of unbalanced rhythms.
Now 56% of the vote is in
and you cry, telling me

it's love but the words sound hollow even to you.
My afternoon anger has turned once more

to sugar-juice.
At least we have gotten past
your being drunk as excuse,
and my saying it's o.k.,
our promises to get through it somehow.

Maybe we won't get through it.
Or maybe we won't get through it together.
We don't deserve these men
grinning through victory signs
anymore than we do the pain
of our own battered histories,
today's careful fear-brimmed lies.

I'm still heading home, our love in my hands.

Albuquerque/New Brunswick, Winter 1986

BE GOOD, SUCCESSFUL, BE AT HOME

for Michael Ratner

Then it was a yankee president, now
it's a hundred million to bring them into line.
Somoza was a son of a bitch
but he was *our* son of a bitch.
Nothing new under the sun.
The few the proud the Marines.
Nicaragua under his skin.
The human nameless in South Africa.
Apartheid the bloody underbelly.
Marcos our honored guest.

Surprise attacks on nations
smaller darker earlier than our own
are all the rage this year.
Sign up, train for pay, you too
can be a mercenary
anywhere in the world today.
This is the family that prays together,
the white picket fence,
what's good for America is good for us.

The judges master 1984, we vote for an actor
and we get an actor.
Batter the dying, govern our bedrooms and our minds,
tremble our hard-won right to choose.
At this the Lady's birthday siege
glitter and be melting pot, be right,
be good, successful, be at home.
Oh be America in battle dress
and sugar-coated plague.

Give us your tired, your poor, your homeless
and their memories.
Nothing new under the sun.
Low intensity warfare
there and here.
Someone just said
we link hands for hunger
and go home to dinner.

Come a long way, baby. Make it safe for death. Rejoice.

Albuquerque, Spring 1986

VIETNAM WAR MEMORIAL

for Jane Creighton

I

One of the Vietnamese who stands with the tall American
and wants his picture taken at the GI statue
looks like Phuc.
Oh but his smile is not the same.
Phuc's smile comes back to me
reflection in a heavy glass table top, 1973.
I am teaching him English. He is teaching me infamy.

In 1974 I went to Vietnam, to the socialist North
and Quang Tri, liberated below the 17th parallel.
That a nation be called by parallels, that a woman gone north
not know of her daughter's life,
that children born in caves squint painfully in light,
that children fear a red T-shirt a red towel the color red,
residue of infamy.

Fifty-eight thousand names, carved in a black granite V.
Fifty-eight thousand individual stories, personal pain
and certainly more to come.
Nicaragua. El Salvador. A moment's wonder
as I note the year: 1959.
Were we there so early? But of course. Advisors
and troops.
Memory pulling itself upright once again.

A scene on a ferry, so small a moment
it's easy to lose.
A woman's face, her eyes
as she asks: where is she from, meaning me,
and my translator answers: America.

61

I will never forget those eyes, that open wound.
There is nothing on this black granite that lies.

America in black granite, 58,000 names,
all of them loved, all remembered.
Again and again they ask: why did you wear that ring?
And again I answer. It was given me
by a woman a peasant woman
in Vietnam.
It was made from the metal of a plane, yes,
an American B-52,
that bombed her village, killing her husband and children.
All of them loved. All remembered.

We hold the infamy on our hands. All of us
hold the infamy on our hands.

II

A name, any name, may be the world.
Touching the contours of its letters
brings spoken and unspoken dreams.
The voiceless dreams must wait.
They are the reasons for this granite wall
this moving line of people.

Mourners closed in sorrow, the curious
with their red white and blue popsicles,
uniformed Rambos, volunteers, children
and those who thrill to morbidity
all walk slowly
leaving flags and flowers, words, objects,
posing for pictures.

You who daily stuff the gaping hole
where small truths break the massive lie,

who will rub your name against this stone?
Tourists with bent memories, generations
trained to forget this was a dirty war for 80% of America.

Nothing on this black granite lies.
We hold the infamy, all of us hold the infamy
on our hands.

Washington DC, June 1986

BLOOD LOOSENS ITS STRANGLEHOLD

"Why is not how . . . it is meaning."
Susan Sherman / *and this poem is for Susan*

My age moves its monthly burden of blood
as opening a book to a particular page, hot and why,
our hands stay where they will
my body stays where it will, waiting.
Blood loosens its stranglehold upon my running feet.

We chose to ignore the writing *and* the wall, the dream
filled our eyes, we didn't want
the commercials.
Somewhere a bell ringing through motionless air
announced a separation of sisters.

We understood that why is not how
beyond words, with a great voice we knew
there is power called creativity
wearing a mask called change.
I know because you taught me this.

All these years beyond placebos filling our mouths,
slivers of glass and sand tearing our feet
we knew beyond mixed messages and no message
beyond heavy rules and doors closed
by others and also by ourselves.

The face that said no the arms that said no the grace
of god or patriarch.
We understood and the island dried our tears.
We stood our ground. We stand our ground.

Albuquerque, Summer 1986

THE MORNING I DREAMED MY CHILDREN

for Audre Lorde

The morning I dreamed my children lingers,
I dreamed them dead,
it was with me morning to morning
and all the nights compressed:
a place of rupture sealed shut.

This morning I came from sleep at five
knowing it was seven where you are, a good time
to start your name on energy waves
my lips to your hospital bed,
a movement of gurneys, hanging bottles, intrusion

their way. Making corrections I whispered
Audre ... Audre ... Audre ... Audre ...
into my sheets, then out onto air, a sound
that would move towards you, take you, hold you,

vibrating from sisters and brothers who know
"we need those who work"
as Sonia said: "those who work ... "
And voices "teach it, sister!" coming from other black women
mostly

and from others of us learning. Learning
to learn.
This morning it was time, one more of our times of trial
and I sang Audre louder

'til the wind caught vowels and they stood
thick fabric of tones swollen for life
Audre ... Audre ...

breaking across my mouth
like the morning I dreamed my children dead. . . and back.

Now their names rise: Gregory . . . Sarah . . . Ximena . . . Ana . . .
Barbara . . . Audre . . . Audre . . . Barbara . . . Francis . . .
and Winnie . . . Guadalupe . . . Dora María . . . Rosa's ghost . . .
the ones who work, oh the ones
who work in me.

Albuquerque, Summer 1987

KALEIDOSCOPE

for my parents,
for my children

My children look out from those sockets,
mother looks away, for a moment father runs
light catching a ridge of gold along his upraised arm.
My own arm rises and falls,
crashes hard against the bed. Raging.

Mother has memory, ideas grow in her garden, voices.
In the time left
she wants to know, doesn't, does.
Custom looms, comfort spins a new dimension, call it
animal vegetable or mineral, this
is no game.

Father insists. I won't forget
how the sun played on the windshield
exactly where and when he told me
how he built and kept a family, ours,
carefully, with honor, inside the thunder,
against desire, against pride.

One fears change, the other blinded by it.

My children's skin so tender to my touch,
I grab the pieces, shards
of mirror spiralling through bone,
its needle-eye.

One fears change, the other blinded by it. Begin again.

Albuquerque, Summer 1986

COATLICUE

My hands coming up for air
survive.
The pulse opens, closes, speaks.
My necklace of skulls is scattered now.
I want to erase your nights
fearing your father's assault
upon your bed, your body.
I want to honor these women who survive. Ourselves.
Honor that part of me
standing tall beneath rain.
When you say I haven't liked myself lately
I want to hold you
turn your face and art
to the mirror of your life.
Make you look. And hold you without limit of time.
I also need to know that the you you do not like is not me
crying in a dark place.
My hands coming up for air, breathe
their own pulse.
The skulls of my necklace have scattered on a heavy sea.
No one should have to sleep
with a baseball bat beneath the sheets.

Albuquerque, July 1986

68

WHAT PART WILL BE SAFE

There's nothing like going to sleep at night
wondering what part will be safe,
where insistence lives,
how they will tell you
they do not ask or even look at you
as if you were whole.

In pieces. Part of the game.
Cut and paste, lock us
in glass files alphabetically tempting
to their appetites. I am not morsel
nor do I grow straight up.
I am not good. Nor even measurable
by their fantasies or games.

And there are times, just before I give myself to sleep
when I wonder about the young ones
or the old not quite brittle in their ways.
How does the rapist feel
constantly lapping another's shoreline,
wetting life's non-linear curve.

I wonder this as I dream, demanding
time to still my muscles, flex my heart
bitten by "the good guys" while the bad sharpen their Bibles,
instruments of torture and of death.

There is nothing, then, farther than morning,
closer than this memory of loss
when we see to, through, beyond
a love that gives and takes, a place to be home.

Albuquerque, Winter 1987

69

FIERCE

*(meditating on the coming
of my first grandchild)*

For years I have wanted the word fierce
to rise in poem, low and sun-filled
in the sky.
Hungering its letters
my tongue probes your waiting heat, breath
coming and going
coming and going
eyes steady in your sudden smile,
a time that will not wait.

Where those other eyes mark time, where
they should not be,
where they die we run and walk, I'm here
with my battle cry, my silence,
here with my comfort arm
when dreams blur, wind grows cold
against my breast.

Fighting this Man's law, fierce
does battle with loss upon this map.
Closing no door, sealing no promise.
Hold me my tongue your broken fire,
proud hands
proud need.
Fierce I am pulling your sound behind me
among elbows, in fingers, on our knees.

Sing it, I will sing it
through the fearful time.
I will wake it at night, let it sleep

by day.
Fierce of place and memory, sky brightening
into song, color on its wings.
For years I have conjured this word
indelible where shadows meet.

For years I have beckoned fierce against fear,
your knowing part, our place
inside this spiral flight.

Albuquerque, Winter 1987

LISTENING

Listening to Kate Wolf, her Poet's Heart
and she dead of leukemia. Just days.
How powerful a voice becomes
when the woman is no longer.

Listening to Kate, and coming across
Joan's cancer journal
her last two years gone five, her words
lost to me until today. Dear Joan.

Where have you been
when I needed you? Where were we Liz
when we needed each other
and could not give, nothing to give,
this cruel certainty stubborn like salt
between us.

No one handed me your death
four days past my intentional last visit
but I knew. You came gently, the confirmation
taking no one by surprise.

Last night I dreamt of death.
Sudden, blatant, jarring.
And when I searched for morning's meaning
(sensing it on some other plane)
someone told me "you can't make death
a synonym for anything else."

I can. Yes I can. And I do
choose to say now
death builds a bridge, another
and one more.

Death builds bridges
as long as we still hear
the living words, the song.

Albuquerque, Winter 1986

MY OTHER COUNTRY

> " . . . writers have to have two countries, the one
> where they belong and the one in which they live
> really. The second one is romantic, it is separate
> from themselves, it is not real but it is really
> there."
>
> —Gertrude Stein

I have walked the streets in cities
in countries where every spoken word
melted into every other spoken word.
Where the signs and signals, small cries,
even the whip of anger
cracked unknown about me.
Code
or wallpaper.
Meaning is mutation, then,
the presence of strangeness. Me, or them.

Behind the window of a moving car
I have traced streets I might not see again
for many years. Or ever.
I have moved conscious of that silent parting
dangling as if from strings
fingered by giant hands
the strongest presence that passive mode:
being moved, *being* led away,
as if my own feet would not go
one before the other, self-sure.

I have stood my ground, accused, punished,
memory-snared, scant place for process,
nothing real
in the system's webbed feet,

it's *country right or wrong.*
We are only as full as we are,
as empty as we wish to be.
And we *do* choose choice,
knowledge not born with birth
but learned.

As I conjure the dream
its surface grows a coat: doubt's weave.
A boundary has been moved
not out of grace
but out of failure.
Voices will tell you
it is yours, *your* failure,
something to call your own
as in: *you've come a long way, baby* . . .
No room for the question, then,
no room for winter's gentle coat.

I will live in both countries
only as long as the journey,
until the new day, only.

Albuquerque, Hartford, Albuquerque
Spring 1987

NORMAL

*. . . Parks Commisioner Stern said one factor in the
tragedy may have been the way bears are
"romanticized by American popular culture. All
bears are not warm, cuddly creatures," he said.
"They like meat a lot more than they like honey."*
(newspaper clipping)

One official response: "the bears
reacted normally."
One small boy, dead.
Eleven-year-old body
size of seven or eight
easily slid between the bars.
Normal? Undernourished

as normal (some never make it
to eleven).
Two bears dead
in normal captivity? Tearing
at an undersized body, normally?
Mother bear, normally dividing the food . . .

We inhabit a world
where normal no longer wears its own clothes.

Philadelphia/Albuquerque - Summer 1987

GO WITH YOUR LIFE, THE WATER SAYS

for Trisha Franzen

This place you have come to
holds minutes of what happened here
so long ago.
The Niagara River still separating nations,
man-made borders.

Now you look across this river
to a foot-path
where pieces of your child's death
sound above today's map.
A life that was and a life that is

fight for center stage, rush
to your eyes, you ask them
to stop for a moment
stop cluttering this image,
please stop.

Just once you want it all to cease:
temperature, movement of water,
the beat of your own heart.
You must find what you search for,
and put it to rest.

In the city buffalo spirits
dance on land you cannot let go of
even on this day that remembers,
holiday-like,
those who leave without formal goodbyes.

But if you blot out water
nothing has happened here. If you cancel sun and rock
memory fades with them.
If you ignore this ache deep in your body
time will not stand upright.

On the Niagara River it's all or nothing
now as then.
All or nothing
as you turn from this place,
fresh pain eating skin, muscle, bone.

Go with your life, the water says,
care for today's map.
Keep on pushing the man-made borders
and I will hold your child here
on memory's face.

Albuquerque, Summer 1987

CONTROL

If she watched the good cowboys
and the bad injuns
on a screen that entered her mind and stayed
you may believe that mirrors cut her Indian face.
Light brown, she passed.
Latina, only her English syllables survived.
A woman, she was as much a man as any man
then as much of a woman was left to her to know.
A story emerged in shoulders like her own.
Woman-loving, she didn't exist
until she invented herself.

If she slouches now
you may be sure she was told to sit up
more than once. And that it was important.
If she always agrees,
we are correct in imagining
things were not what they seemed.
Not what they seemed to be
at all.

At a table of broken manners
she sits before a plate piled high
of rancid food.
There is gravy in her hair.
She practised hard at being agreeable
so only smiles weakly
when armies of bloated bellies
are hired to do the dishes.
She herself will pay them. In flowers.

When she goes home at last
she will have to take her history

from her pocket,
spit and polish the map,
speak in tongues
and gently insist upon that skin
until anger is born in her eyes,
healing her wounds, turning her flesh
to earth.

Albuquerque, September-October 1985